# EYESHOT

WESLEYAN POETRY

Also by Heather McHugh

*Dangers: Poems* (1977)

*A World of Difference: Poems* (1981)

*D'Après Tout: Poems by Jean Follain* (trans., 1982)

*To the Quick* (1987)

*Shades* (1988)

*Because the Sea Is Black: Poems of Blaga Dimitrova*
   (trans. with Nikolai Popov, 1989)

*Broken English: Poetry and Partiality* (1993)

*Hinge & Sign: Poems, 1968–1993* (1994)

*The Father of the Predicaments* (1999)

*Glottal Stop: 101 Poems by Paul Celan*
   (trans. with Nikolai Popov, 2000)

*Cyclops* by Euripides (trans. 2001)

# EYESHOT

HEATHER McHUGH

Wesleyan University Press
Middletown, Connecticut

Published by Wesleyan University Press, Middletown, CT 06459

Printed in the United States of America
CIP data on last printed page of this book

ISBN 0-8195-6671-3

## ACKNOWLEDGMENTS

*Agni Review:* "Fido, Jolted by Jove" (under the title "Dog, with Due Respect to God") and "Unhygienic Song"

*American Letters and Commentary:* "Boy Thing" (under the title "Felt Would Feel")

*Antioch Review:* "Night Storm"

*Bellevue Literary Review:* "Back to B.C."

*Best American Poetry of 2001:* "Money Minus One" (a section of "The Magic Cube")

*Chicago Review:* "Just Some" (a section of "The Magic Cube")

*Conduit:* "One's Mons" (a section of "The Magic Cube")

*Connecticut Review:* "A Dearth in the Dreamboat Department"

*Electronic Poetry Review:* "Iquity"

*Epoch:* "Letters, Numbers, Signs, Words Referred to as Words"

*Forklift:* "Goner's Boner"

*Harvard Review:* "Songs for Scientists, Parts I and II"

*Heliotrope:* "Significant Suspicions"

*Iowa Review:* "World in a Skirt"

*Kestrel:* "Far Sight," "Settling Song," "Lectator's Song"

*Literary Imagination:* "Affinity Welled"

*Posterband:* "Long Shot with Shutter"

*Provincetown Arts:* "Mind's Eye"

*Slate:* "Retort Room"

*Slope:* "Impolitic"

*Spork:* "Pound Sign"

*Tikkun:* "Fourth of July, B.C."

*Verse:* "Song for a Mountain Climber"

*Web del Sol:* "Sampling"

# CONTENTS

*The eye I see God through is the same eye through which God sees me.*

—Meister Eckhart

*Blindness is . . . a liberation, a solitude propitious to invention, a key and an algebra.*

—Jorge Luis Borges

# WORLD IN A SKIRT

The French horn has us
where she wants us—in a whirl.

We flew around her hem of gold
(a cone blown off a rod): our own 360

sped to one head-turner, sure to sharpen us,
to get the lead out—spin us inward,

get some endlessness involved. (With seven shaven sunshines,
four red top hats, scraps of our leftover everything, still

she cannot get her fill, left right, boy girl, no matter how
she turns herself into us, us into

her eyeshot's veered veneer.) She's only molten
earwear but she's changing

round from noun to adjective and back—
echo into dream-drink,

fixer into flower. One and two and more and less
are wound inside her gown. She welds the sunlights,

sequins squalors, calls beholding's kettle gold. She improvises swells
in every bugle's riverrun: the looks of us pour in, and lo!

the likes of Humperdinck pour out! My god!—my fickleness! (my
centerer of yore!) If every petal's fugal in your sphere,

if every pull's a fling, how can a human being tell
immortal from amoral here? Is love

only cupidity? (In a silver twist,
a spire's unfixed. Now it's a spear.)

# GONER'S BONER

Is it a mistake
or a misgiving?
There he hangs,
though it does not,
that sign of heat and hope.

His neck is roped; his head is hooded: no more
plans in there. His watch is blind, his mind
on hold. Only the arrow from his crotch

could indicate some final wishes.
(Could, but doesn't: this display
is actually adventitious; never mind, it's his
big fifteen minutes.) Forward, but not
forward-looking, in his day
he cursed the present.
Seeing how

unpleasant such
x-ratedness can be,
the onlookers appear
struck dumb. But he—

he's holding sway
against the notion

only good can come.

# FIDO, JOLTED BY JOVE

Your shaking shakes a two-ton truck.
From a Thor whose fury

thunders through a parking lot
how can you hide your hide?

The dark is daggered, windshield pearled and
shafted. (Therefore you have shrunk to fit

the inches between brake and clutch.) The world
itself is worried. Trees stand out, spectacularly

branched: the mind's eye grows alert: this thing
could hurt. It had you once, in a puddle of mud;

and now it's having second thoughts—about
thirteen a minute. Are you trembling

for a reason? (Are you sure?) Just
wait: a brain this insecure may need

another bolt be driven in it.

# SIGNIFICANT SUSPICIONS

Kings and chairmen, ministers and presidents
contend for countrysides. One wonders
about all that one envisions:

all that one. One's hold on everything,
one's whole will-hold. Shrunk to a dot
in a field of dotted swiss,
pin-prick in a cheap
French letter, shot
of rue from Bourbon Street, or
ooze from Easy, you essay

to go on. You go on. But Rome will burn
before you learn to fiddle. Rings
your fingers might have loved will only
discompose your nose. You dream of Rose and her
revisions: you get glasses. Men who should be saying "I for one

am sorry for the things I've done" have been assigned instead
to say somebody's masses. Shop girls will not profit from
the rabble-rouser's holier-than-thou. It's close to home

the far gleam hits: the sun (your own be-all-and-end-all)
scatters into glitter, hints of scat: the coin and hubcap,
foil from Lucky Strike and stings from jar,
or old ardented ear-rings . . . Oddly, one

lives on, continually torn
between the two significant suspicions:
on the one hand that in all the scheme of things we matter
marvelously little; on the other, that we *are*

the scheme of things.

# FOURTH OF JULY, B.C.

Each evening brings its modicum
of glitter to the nation. But this one is the work
of some uncommon pyrotech: the blue and scarlet biospheres
blown up and then flown off—the people left
in dazzling dandelion-drift . . . by dint of which

the topical becomes the typical again,
the shimmer just a shine. (Did I imagine them?
Those flashy chemistries and colored concentrations
twenty miles across the sea, were they
just eye-salts, mind-motes, practice
for an aneurysm? Blink, and proud
America comes down

to dust and asterisks.)
But there, above
Port Angeles,
unmoved,

is sheer
Olympic imperturbability—a hundred
times a township's height, an impassivity attended by
impressive skies of its own manufacture. Men had best
beware: the price of its ascent is steep:
the peak of its indifference

is monumental, unrelated to the flags we've chosen
from our local five-and-ten. The mountain's root
is fire; the mountain's flower frost:
our thoughts won't keep

inside its ken. A final poof!
and men are scattered

into manyness again. . .

# UNHYGIENIC SONG

They love us, don't they, louse and gadfly,
centipede and roach? The cabinet that has the mouse

will have the twice-accommodated fleas: they
room here in the dreamhouse, ruminating as

they please. A host may take them for the most
unpalatable pals; but they're not hurt. You'll see

which critters disappear when humankinds approach:
the nobler ones, not these. Our habits are their habits,

and our waste their luxuries. They don't despise us:
Rather fondly they inspect our wakes and sleeps;

re-comb what we would leave behind, become
the company we keep. (Their host is not

beneath them yet—and yet he's not dependably
above. That is the one American

condition of the love.)

## LETTERS, NUMBERS, SIGNS,
## WORDS REFERRED TO AS WORDS

They set themselves aside
from ordinary words;
they never could conceive
a spirit outside language.
Nightly, nonetheless, it slips
like breeze through gauze
into the human room
where, under her

dissertative crib-sheet, lies
the baby of means—tricked out
in deep REM sleep and blue-veined
birthday suit—that suit with feet. (Somebody
made this baby! or—according with the laws—
some double body, whose coherent thoughts

burst into hot red asterisks one night. Ten times since then
the pepper trees have turned; the mother's best material
dissolved; some say the zebra has divorced
her partner in the alphabet, the scurrilous
antelope, who with the deer
and buffalo has played. There's love,
and then there's love. The cross is cross;

the bloodletters have razorblades.)
When nursery curtains billow, is it
spirit, or a virus? Tell us true. (It ought
to be a breeze.) The mirror sets its trap for two

completely decent moons.
"On nights like these,"

the dashes whisper
to the ampersands,


"Thank God our plurals take apostrophes."

# BOY THING

I.

A stretch of school,
a stretch of temple,
pupils trained to tell

such parts apart: those were the days when we
could be drawn forth, by definition, by the masterminds;
drawn on, drawn in, aired out, as through a pipe's
brain-stem. But once the boys took aim
you could not hear the melody above

the roar of sys- and diastole,
an eminence less gray than red.
(It rakes the mind's ear and abrades
an idea's door. What storms does love devise,

to sideswipe reason! One quick fork
to the cerebellum's underbelly,
two sharp lops to the
foremost lobes—
and just like that—chop! chop!—
all history was fast repast, rewined, redowned!—

like gobbled seconds on a bad blind date,
so many snacks for the sex cyclops).


II.

Sight makes noise—annoying
the recovered blind. It sponsors far
too much detail (exhaustive is exhausting!).
Had I, my whole life long, been given only
smell, to know you by, I might resent today

this gift of touch, despite the sweet planes
of your long beloved back. With musk
so mesmerizing, felt would feel gloved.

Lower and lower the lover goes
into the blue medulla, where
a mere iota throws the whole
shebang awry. (Even the big baleens
spend all their living daylights filtering
some tiny phytoflagellates.) A baby puts in
time and a half, but cannot sort
a minor from a major

premise. I myself
am boggled; time lines seeming
so elaborately mirrored, act three
turning to scene two in beveled revelry,
the future to the past, and res for res, ponding for cueing.
All the more crying for brain-noise; all the more

aching for doing. (No wonder, given a heaven,
we incline to echo chambers;
given the chance
of a lifetime,

wind up toys.)

# THE MAGIC CUBE

## I.

The taxonomy comes free with the unit.
The unit comes free with the wrench.
The wrench comes free with
the hand. The hand comes
(monkey with me, said
the header) under the
pen-man's custody.

## II.

It's just some
monad's morning, Monday
minus sex. (You take YY: now there's
a carrier.) Oh man in the air, oh mom
in the moon-milk. (God, your zip code
keeps eluding me. Oh one,
oh one, oh one. Hex-

agonad, you're pent-up plus.
You aren't just number, or most numb,
like any bombast gas's additive—
your metric is comparatively
uncontainable, your come
is emanations and
your weep a throe.

Spare us a sea, spare us a sec, or simply
spare us. Ever and ever
to be, your future's our
infinitive, a pure
impossibility.)

III.

My one
and only: money
minus one. No noun
like a pronoun!—best of all
the jealous kind. Come, come,
company doll, cide with a coin,
one moan, one
more, honey
bunch.

# IMPOLITIC

Into the soothing sound-proofed hundred-powered
air of SUV and cruise ship cream there comes
the clop of the fetlocked one, the blinkered mare, the one

who carriages her way along the docks, past mansioned points
and pollardings of park (in short, wherever seaside seers
care to steal a scene, or four, or more, for

pocket-cameras, steal an hour, or half,
or less, from pocket-watches, talk
talk talking as they go). But dallying is what she

doesn't do, who has to drag them,
sometimes five or six obesities
down Dallas Road, to where

she's hinted with a whipper's lick
to turn (at Turner: here
the clopping's altered,

clipped, a swift decision
brought to bear—she has to cross
oncoming chrome—a will is rallied,

wherewithal applied.) And then the corner
braved and left behind, the lower
slower pockmarks settle back,

distinctly four,
from which
the balconist's

unholidaying ear picks up
the oddity for which it was alert:
the quirk of individuation, twist

of hand or tendency of hoof,
discernible at last above
the scenic generality:

for one
most clearly (more
than all or some) will hurt.

# THE RETORT ROOM

It had tottered for years on the water's
lip and lap. Some squatter-pigeons occupied its nights,
dreaming of drowning in glottals. Then suddenly

the trucks arrived and hauled away
enormous rusted remnants of
the cannery's cookery. Inside a week,

the great stained concrete that had poured down
fifty years and twenty feet into the tide
was sheathed up pink in plywood someone

trundled from a lumberyard. The whole place bloomed
in polyester greenery and sky-blue styrofoam.
And sure enough, from farther south,

with a flourish of romance and a big RV,
he brought his wife of decades here to live
in dreamland—dead end of the island's

eastmost street, so he could twinkle, she abide.
The bright new retort room (where once upon a time
the cans were boiled) now bore his masterwork: nailed

near the Wal-Mart welcome sign, a home-made
six-foot jigged-out replica of tug, as jaunty as you like
(the city cousin of the working ones

that chug along the waterside.) It was his bid at
immortality. We liked him more, the more he tried.
He beamed past every tiredness of a day (retired

by choice!), past eking out, past aching in. He shone
like someone past the past, with whom resides
what conquers all. And that was when she died.

# SAMPLING

When the table is turned, the hand
resists: it's a drag—then suddenly

it's a rhythm section. Needlestick of stimulant
for some two-timing touch; a centrifuge for

boost and beat. (It burns to move, it turns the tunes
to hiccup-arts all down the street.) Such feline

felonies! Such licks of scratch!—insinuated
into sitting rooms, where someone's upright

grandma thinks of love—and gets
amen, a mensch, a mention—

(all because bad vinyl snagged
the handyman's attention . . .).

# LECTATOR'S SONG

The first taste killed us, so
we wanted it again. The second

mated with the minute: taste took
time, it seemed, and so required the mind

to mind the tongue, stop being young,
start being tired. The future had

retiring in it: and the wrist a little
drum. (A present with a bow, a girl

could come, apparently, from anywhere—
from calm gene-pools or panic-stricken

pulling-off of pants. Nobody has a
snowball's chance—of staying her, or staying

here—one sea-spark in a million.) Still, devices
give delight. That cat-o'-nine-tails has some life

left in it. Give us, gods, just
three licks more. (For who

forgoes, for long—or could!—
O sires, o cadences!—your near

annihilating prefix?)

# FAR SIGHT

*Victoria, B.C., fall 2001*

The sea is a far sight from
a friend. Into a cauldron under a cloud
the sun pours out its heart. Along a shining baseline
several mountains nurse a haze. But every other
reconciling's shot: even the sea-beasts have

been fooled, in twisted scarves and
staved-off airs.
                  The sea is not malicious,
but it's cold. From aft to mid to fore,
unmoving on a moving deck,
the young men rise and fall to the

occasion of the news, and blink back
sun-dust, or a fear. . . . From shore we lift
our handkerchiefs; the warship passes
into boiling gold, and then, in our
purview, turns black.

What the sea can't love
it purifies. To heaven it sends
a billion winking *billets doux:*

*I've eyes for you, I'm coming back.* . . .

# IQUITY

It too has a den.
(In all the best democracies

we watch TV.) And any child of time
(whose father is a big bête noir)

desires to have his looks averted
from unpleasant likelihoods.

But still Red Ridings by the hundreds could not
cuddle one bad night away, while in the den

the Buddha seems a giggle-meister. Dr. Factoid
sells some fish oil: fewer suicides in

Matsushima. Action, faction: subtlety be sacked.
The den is Poll Land: let's just get along!

Unhappy endings outlawed by a
scientific vote! No need for misery: in cine-pop

a little extra nookie on the side; in cine-mom your
hubbie hurries home. (Hi, hon.) Your honor, honest,

is not implicated. Soothers
must, by definition, say

no terrifying truths. And mercy knows
what men have done!—(that's why the one

and only split. They quit. The universal
donor is a goner).

# FOUR COMMISSIONS

## SONGS FOR SCIENTISTS, PARTS I AND II
*In memoriam J.L.M.*

### I. BRAIN COLLECTOR AT CORNELL

Unhelmeted, formaldehyded, plopped
into their seven separate jars,
the seven human brains appear
immodestly exposed. But no,

they won't give up their privacy.
Grown in a bone bin, now not one of them
can let go of the knot at its gut, the fruit
of its last thought. The sheer detachment's

absolute. Was it you, placed all these
bare brains in a row, so they would face (so
to speak) one way? Below, at the workspace,
a jar is agape. And there you are, as if in love—

*in flagrante delicto,* a hunch in the flesh,
alive, in your scientist suit—O single-minded
one!—with glaring head and glasses and
a handful of sensation's plunder! Do you

prod for God's address? grope to learn
if love survives? hope to know if thunder's
good? The seven skies
contain themselves,

their brainstorms
dimly understood.

## II. ORNITHOLOGUE AT AUDUBON

Given a simple flycatcher, you forked
or scissored it. You sorted birds by
adjective (you marbled a godwit, shafted a flicker,
leasted a grebe) and soon the sky itself seemed

liable to fall into rubrics. That's when someone dreamed
this other occupation up: to set your snares
for love songs, by the bowerside and brook—
and bring, as if they were theirs, your own

callings, back to the birdbook—where, to
this day, any fool who reads can find
the wingèd singing things distinguished
chiefly by their expertise in English. Take

the goldfinch. What peculiar flight of fancy
made it say "Potato chips!"? Hadn't it a higher sort
of calling to its name? (Or were you, Sir, by any chance,
annuitized by Lay's?) You claim a dove inquires

"Who cooks for you?"—(it seems the birds
are food-obsessed); another specimen is heard
to squawk out "Quick! Three beers!"—and soon
the vireo appears impatient too, snapping "Quick,

quick, give me the raincheck!" The woods are thick
with poet-types and pollyannas, pleased-to-meetcha
greeters, segue artists gone from food to mood with a chip-
chip-chipper or a sweet-sweet-sweet. One bad Wordsworth

specializes in the "Trees, trees, murmuring
trees." The masochists are even worse, the pessimists,
tenors from hell—the plover's disheartening
"Quit quit quit," the inca dove's "No hope,"

and thugs who keep on hissing
"Whip Tom Kelly"—God! what's left
for a thrasher to do, whose utterance you render simply
"one sharp smack?" (To a lover's mind, I guess,

that's more or less a kiss. You must have loved
as much as punished them—you did not miss
the courting eider's human-sounding moan, nor, among
warblers, the black-throated blue's own "please me, please

please squeeze me!"). Estimable Sir, desist! Were you
delirious? or lonely? maybe married? (Were you
unacquainted with the word *displacement*?) Translators
are ever undersung. But mark my words, some serious

misanthropomorphizing got done
to the hapless chachalaca—best of birds,
the one whose amorous aptitudes
fell into permanent doubt

when its females were quoted to cry "Keep it up!"—
and its males to reply "Cut it out."

# SONG FOR THE MEN OF THE PENNSYLVANIA HILLS


It was not because the heavens
didn't shine upon the match
nor for want of indication
that he thought himself a catch.

He was able, he was stable
as a Harvard running back;

of the requisite credentials
there was surely not a lack.

Lack of coulda? Lack of shoulda?
Lack of spermicidal foam? No,
it was just for Lackawanna
that I didn't take him home.

# SONG FOR A MOUNTAIN CLIMBER

Since fondness is rooted in folly,
shouldn't we should pray
that God's indifferent? Beyond
the fawning flock, past Everest and air,

shouldn't he stay a wholly yawning
dark? (The orders of indifference
more mightily amaze than those
of love. Love favors; love

excludes. On a lark, love tries
its millstone; on a sky its tint.
Love takes an object, takes a shine
to a calf whose gold its own eye-smitheries

have minted. Pure indifference
moves otherwise. It's unconditional:
a little fling cannot diminish it:
impartially it flies from everything—

from man's investments, and
his dearth.) The thought that God

might care for us is
terrifying: ought

to keep us hooked on earth.

# MANKIND'S PET, THE COPYCAT

1

One man's female article
is another man's bone: and it takes two

to really roll. (My my.) Her favorite snakes
possess apiece

one itsy-bitsy eye. (His beaver
features wisdom teeth, inside a big bad

cold.) You're your
own owner, no?

2

Attention now. We have
a bulletin straight

from the underworld.
Murderous starfish are

feeding on reef.
(Your reef, being alive,

can give your starfish
awful adjectives.)


3

Slipping from a verb into something
more comfortable, our old friend Being

yearns to multiply. (One cannot live without
its colony. But colonies themselves can

move and mate, make tracks of scat, and then
what's one to be? Sub-nuclear? an up-and-coming

former family? an imminence, or an infinitive?
All one. All gone.) There's air


4

in them thar bubbles. (Rising from the critic,
don't they smack of something sunk? A Maker, maybe.

Or Forsaker, if he's any kin of ours. Ephemera appear
perpetual to us, who read the world by eye-gulp, eye-gloss,

pupil-race and spot-lit blind.) Somebody spell us! Help!
The ducks should duck, the hollers howl, the wind

round up that rustling band—the one that calls
itself Itself.

# FOUR POEMS AFTER THE CHINESE

## AFTER SU TUNG P'O

ON THE BIRTH OF A SON

When a child is born, the parents say
they hope it's healthy and intelligent. But as for me—

well, vigor and intelligence have wrecked my life. I pray
this baby we are seeing walloped, wiped and winningly anointed,

turns out dumb as oakum—and more sinister. That way
he can crown a tranquil life by being

appointed a cabinet minister.

## AFTER LI BAI

You ask how I can bear it there
in the wild, in the mountains—and minus
amenities! Take for adequate reply
my smile: I'm out of the whole damn fray!

The fallen flower flows
downstream—but where? No one can say.
From the world of destinations mine
is a whirling world away.

## AFTER WANG WEI

An unspoiled mountainside: no person can be seen.
Just now and then you hear the human voices.
One sun-ray settles
into deepest green—

reflecting more than once upon the mosses.

## AFTER SU TUNG-P'O

One midnight in the spring! An hour
is worth a thousand golden coins . . .
The moon is shadowed, senses
clearly flowering. Upstairs,
unwound from flutes and
thoats—some silken
threads of sound.
And where the
garden holds
most still:
a swing.

# TWO TUNES FOR ELLIOT

## AFFINITY WELLED

from color to color, shape to shape. A purple burning overspilled
the porch-side torches of the lilac—then went on to lupine
whole innocent hillsides. To one old sea-salt of
seducer whirlpool, two sea-sidlers took
their shines and turns.
Coincidence

is not an accident. It surfaces in order for the eye
(and its possessive mind) to love. Above a kind
of island is its kind of cloud. Above
a bend, a limb: tree whip or tanner
of a lady's man, the blown
day's glee. The seal

(you do—you did—agree) may swerve first one
and then another way, but never is he hesitant.
He swerves because the whirlpools do, two
times a day, one hour before
the floodtide. Thus
affinities

affirm themselves: from time
to time. I (happening to be
alive—or feeling
alive, feeling a-
round—a
fool

for feeling!) found
you fond as well,
o fellow soul,

just one
swell
shy

of me. . . .


## ONE'S MONS


The moon has one, and the thumb of the man
in the moon has one, and a mind
of its own in the thumb of the man
has one un-single-minded one,
and wooing has

a way to win a landscape over,
waving has a handsome sea, a many-
fingered, many femurred evening, has
a night and a day to wave away—a woe to
revamp and a man to rewoo, and a day
and a night were only the

umpteenth.

# BACK TO B.C.

Streaming, striped with
blown snow-smoke, the
highway ran at odds with
wind the whole of Man-
itoba and Saskatchewan.
The trouble was the truck

took broadside dispositions
from the wind; the eye
(which drove the mind's
attention to the road)
was now forever being teased
from its intents and constancies.
(Otherwise, weatherless, it would
have been at one with all

the strictland flats of Middle West
macadam. Here instead, in twists
and tails, to find its wits consorting
with the mist!—this little was
too much! The brightest roadlines
disappeared.) The mind is made
to discipline the eye so that the eye
can aim the mind—or else
the troubled vision thinks

I know my own way home, I'll show
these whippersnappers what a looker is . . . .

❧

But then the landscape did
let up, its sweep diverted

into big and little vortices by
foothills: dark and highland
sorts of snow

began to dim
the enterprise. The truck's
own motion in the midnight drove,
by pointillistic billions, into eyeshot,
sycophants the host was both
attracting and attracted to.
(Mis-matcher or
mote-mesmerizer,
specialist in quirk,

the mind's impressionism always runs
the risk of masterwork.)

You think you're home free,
coasting down the coastal side? Think twice, think more—
no polymath can think enough. The ultimate seduction lies
before you, in a temperate domain,

along a trail you trust, just
hours short of home's familiar shift,

where Sleep Incorporated veers across your path—
to silverize your dust,

to destinize your drift . . .

# NIGHT STORM

In a flash, in pure detail, mind-boggling
miles unfurl, each inch of the endless
world (out of no mere mean-
whiled sense of time) is
branded by eye on
brainpan. Wow.

What whirlpools full of futuristic mercury! What
islands reprimanded on what neuroscopic
forks, with fractals tilled for sheer
bezillions' sake! Assailed as
Cronus, I'm at once
awake. Hit me

Again, you old degenerate! From everydimsday
turn me in, and into sizzling imminence again.
(Who hate from habit learn from lack:
the seven dailies, thirty journals
could be jolted, brainchild:
fuse the five refusers!)

While you're at it, wire a song into the bargain.
Men may drone on, intermittencies permit.
But let the minders (screwed in their
stead, bolted in their sleep) be
by the vault's live deep
revolted.

# MIND'S EYE

The moon zooms in
on strands of negligee—
it has a mind to be webbed
in neurostrata and stigmata.

Lower in our purview, torrents
tear across the floodgate's crossbar, where
what *was* turns fast into what *is*. How shallowly I loved!
The streaking downticks at the shine-slide mean

an outcome of upended quiver.
There against the tide arise
some greenblack blades,
a row athrob. The falls
are brawling, mob of suds, mud
in your eye. I may well
burn to fly, but light

has its own bent. Downline, it's not
our substance pours away:
it is our shine.

# A DEARTH IN THE DREAMBOAT DEPARTMENT

The surface's dilemma: no fact being bare, the faces
everywhere winking, the drink just one big drop.

So a pine slides down to a seafold, a freehold
of facets, all my ownerships and signage not-

withstanding.  Kin and kith keep
dying off, and off and on,

the ones with all my faces and
the one with all my heart. (Don't

start. And still
don't end. Take

numbers, or sedators, or
a motor, if you must.) All homes

are moving, even posted ones.
That's utterly unsettling, god

above! We thought you'd thing along.
Instead you thunder us: it's only

woe, woe, woe your boat. Warily,
warily. It's not fair. We need a breeze,

we get a gust. We need a love, you give
a damn: a surface lust. A scream from

time to time, a stab in the
glissando. Life is just—

is what?—is just?

# VOICEBOX

In a moment one looks up, unable to remember.
In a month the nomenclatures overcoat the number.

Time's to fly, and kings to fall. The rest of us must wait
An eon to retire. We checked our Fahrenheit.

The legend comes to life: I thought he'd kicked the book
O moons ago. (I'd missed a period, our love was late, looks

Fell to me from that full pail.) In other words one cannot overstate
The case for removing a downhearted noun. Just operate

Face-first: the ticker takes forever. Cells the size of fists;
Close calls in rest rooms; far cries in caves. Must we exist

In pro and retrospect? Arrive again at this
Enormous minute? Evermore be made to miss

The last words in it?

# POUND SIGN

*In memoriam Elliot Fishbein*

1

She was dropping voluminous numbers
of books and backpacks on me, bathing towels and
children's jackets . . . Suddenly she saw a body

suffocating underneath—and dug me out.
She rocked me sympathetically for hours.
"You get no rest," she said.

2

You're right. You're right.
When I lie in the sand,
it's with clenched fists;
when I'm deepest in sleep,
the whole night long, I'm thinking

Do not be mistaken!
you're awake.

3

I'd been carrying a corpse on my back forever,
in that bag. I knew it the way you know
you are alive. At last at a tree
I could stop, and actually

open up the sack.

The body's fingernails were tinily inscribed
with symbols, letterforms and ideograms, and all
in exquisite detail. I looked and looked,

I looked my grown-up sight away,
forgot the worlds I hadn't seen to,
couldn't read—but knew the signs

I wouldn't need to.

# LONG SHOT WITH SHUTTER

Through coordinates of windowsash and intersection
(twenty-four per second) pour
the molten car-flow, human hurry . . .

I can't stop it, being the
bearing of blur.

Those oaks would be my kind of live
if I saw years-an-animated-minute. Concrete vaults
would fasten down, if I had decades in a flash. The fixed and flowing
indistinct, the world might not be lovable. And yet—and yet—

and yet we love.

(But does our subject
matter? As long as we live,
as headlong as we like, we feature it,
so it will feature us.) O will, unable to contain
this cursive, this subversive currency!—O will,
sweet will, why be so self-consoled inside

the diocese of perishing,
through which are wound and whiled away

our streams of creature?

# SETTLING SONG

*For my mother*

One who could fly
from the rose-closed deck
toward starfuls, farthest-flung, of pure

forgetful sky might take
the forks and tributaries in the night—
afar, aloft—only to find

herself mistaken: nothing upward
ever brings her nearer.
Land's alluring after all, from there,

its oil fields quietly constellatory,
suburbs subtled by abounding glow. . . .
And so a soul might settle back

toward the old dim beck
of bedside, one shade shy
of wicked glimmers. There to

bide and be. In sight
of the flicker of living.
In spite of the quicker to die.

# THROUGH

*After Sully Prudhomme*

In blue or black, all lovely and beloved,
Some countless human eyes have seen the dawn.
They're sleeping at the bottom of the grave.
Here comes the sun.

But far more delicately than the days
The nights ignite in countless eyes a spark.
The stars are always sending out their rays:
Eyes fill with dark.

That they should lose their glimmer, one and all—
No way. It simply isn't possible.
I say they've turned toward the side we call
Invisible.

And like the stars that must incline to set
They too are somewhere out there in the sky;
The eye-lights may go down at times and yet
They do not die.

All lovely or beloved, in black and blue,
To any dawn's immensities disposed
On earth's far side they're seeing through
The lids we closed.

# BLIND MEN

*After Charles Baudelaire*

Just look at them, my soul. Are they not
Truly awful? Alien as mannequins, a little
ludicrous. Solitary, creepy. Walkers in their sleep.
Training those darkened globes on God knows what.

Their eyes (from which the spark of the divine
is missing) tilted upward, as if seeing far-off matters.
(Never are their heavy heads inclined to downward gazing,
dreaming in the gutter.) Heads held high, they pass us by,

and pass an everlasting night, the kin
of everlasting silence. City! Centrifuge
of brawl and roar, you whirl your horns and songs
about me, avid unto sheer atrocity, while I must haul

this carcass of my own around, beneath such skies
as man can bear—and wonder (far more mystified
than they): what are those blind guys always
*looking* for, up there?

# OUT OF EYESHOT

Years I poured it forth, without
a thought. To left and right

I sprayed the wide world's
spectacle. I made a blue

bird sparkle, and a red tree;
phones rang under my auspices,

then an ocean, buckling by the
bucketful: its whole ferocity

was facets. Shorelines shivered
at the sights of me, before which

cities too had been delivered: a van
with a dent to its name; a rack of near-

dead ringers, rolled in an alleyway; and men
I had glanced in their tracks. Just take a little

shine, a tiny tearburst, and you blow
coherences to rainbows. Who needed

aim? I had an instrument.

But now I'm down to two rounds more.
The looks things level at my gaze

are lit with far more animus than
anima—a gang of gongs. (I have to dodge

the ricochets.) A single gray would suit me fine—
instead I'm shot to green-red smithereens. If just

to have a salvo dry (for what's in store—
the big shebang) I cannot weep. I keep

my head. I do not make a scene.

# THE SUICIDE

*After Jorge Luis Borges*


Not a single star will be left in the night.
The night will not be left.
I'll die and, when I do,
I will annihilate the whole
unbearable universe: destroy
the pyramids, erase the honorary medals,
wipe out every countenance and continent. I'll do away
with the accumulated past, make dust of history,

dust of dust. I'm watching the final sunset,
I'm listening to the last bird's note.

I'm leaving nothing to no one.

# THE LOOKER

I was as dead as I could be, and you
weren't there. They held a big glass
up to me; they blocked the world with
their lifelonging. What they wanted was

a cloud (the kind that tells the living of
themselves). But I was well past telling.
I was a looker at last, head back, mouth wide
as in a heat or holler. (I had always looked

my best astonished. With a nose as close to its chin
as this, what aesthete would be caught dead with
her mouth shut? It's a matter of the golden mean.
But then the aesthete knows—who cannot shut her mouth—

she'd better find the finest words around: a matter of
the golden rule. No faking, no mistaking. Only real
love-moans, and wonders un-translatable. No
sweat. When you're as dead as this, you're not

a cheat or chatterbox.) Don't fear to look. Don't look
to stay. Given the almost-clear, the near-
unclouded glass, I did what you
weren't there to do.

I took my breath away.

# NOTES

"The Magic Cube": The Magic Cube was James Joyce's favorite brothel in Trieste.

"Songs for Scientist, Parts 1 and 2" was commissioned by the Phi Beta Kappa for delivery at its graduation ceremony, Harvard University, June 2000.

"Song for the Men of the Pennsylvania Hills" was commissioned by my father, shortly before his death. He liked his poems rhyming, ribald, and readily understood.

"Song for a Mountain Climber" was commissioned by the University of Washington in 1999, in celebration of a much-publicized prospective $2 million endowment for its extraordinary MFA program. When the endowment did not materialize, the UW's poetry situation was materially worsened, since other (more honorable) donors, believing its future assured, turned their philanthropic attentions elsewhere.

"Mankind's Pet, the Copycat" was commissioned by the Getty Museum in Los Angeles for delivery at a 2001 colloquium on replicas, facsimiles, reproductions, and fakes.

# ABOUT THE AUTHOR

The author of six books of poetry, including the National Book Award finalist *Hinge & Sign,* Heather McHugh has been named a chancellor of the Academy of American Poets and a fellow of the American Academy of Arts and Sciences. She is the recipient of awards from institutions such as the National Endowment for the Arts, PEN, and the Guggenheim foundation. McHugh earned her B.A. from Harvard University and her M.A. from the University of Denver. She is currently the Milliman Distinguished Writer-in-Residence at the University of Washington and a regular visitor at the fabled low-residency MFA Program for Writers at Warren Wilson College in Asheville, North Carolina.

Library of Congress
Cataloging-in-Publication Data

McHugh, Heather, 1948–
    Eyeshot / Heather McHugh.
        p. cm. — (Wesleyan poetry)
    ISBN 0-8195-6671-3 (alk. paper)
        I. Title.    II. Series
PS3563.A311614E94 2003
811'.54—dc21            2003053526